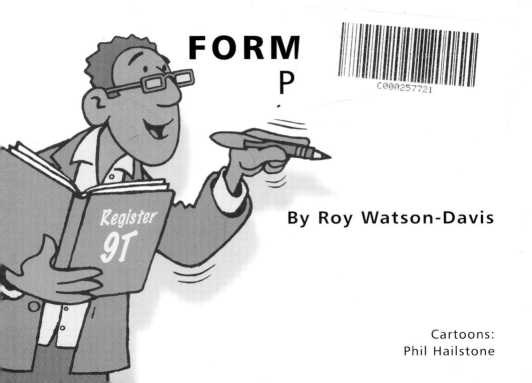

FORM

P

By Roy Watson-Davis

Register 9T

Cartoons:
Phil Hailstone

Published by:

Teachers' Pocketbooks
Laurel House, Station Approach,
Alresford, Hampshire SO24 9JH, UK
Tel: +44 (0)1962 735573
Fax: +44 (0)1962 733637
E-mail: sales@teacherspocketbooks.co.uk
Website: www.teacherspocketbooks.co.uk

*Teachers' Pocketbooks is an imprint of
Management Pocketbooks Ltd.*

Series Consultant: **Brin Best**.

© Roy Watson-Davis 2005.

This edition published 2005.

ISBN 1903776 69 4

British Library Cataloguing-in-Publication
Data – A catalogue record for this book is
available from the British Library.

Design, typesetting and graphics by Efex Ltd.
Printed in UK.

Contents

Introduction

A key role in any school is that of form tutor. As a form tutor you are asked to lead the development of your students, instil into them good habits and routines, support colleagues in their attempts to educate and discipline your tutees, and act as some kind of uber counsellor as you guide your form through a wide range of social challenges. Yet, for this you receive very little training, with the role too often treated as some kind of minor 'bolt on' to subject teaching, something you can happily (and miraculously) pick up as you go along. The purpose of this book is to redress this imbalance, outline the key areas of the job, and to act as a practical guide to support you in the role.

With the current move to use non-teaching staff in pastoral roles, this book will also be useful if you are coming to tutoring from a different perspective, perhaps as a learning mentor or teaching assistant.

What Do They Want from Me?

The big picture

Within a school, the form tutor's role is exciting and positive because it is dynamic. What started out largely as an administrative role involving taking registers and reading out notices, has evolved into something far more central to raising student achievement and looking after their welfare. As pastoral concerns gained a higher profile, the form tutor took on more specific issues linked to social development, often delivering PSHE material as an essential part of their job. In some schools this was extended further, the tutor embracing citizenship issues linked to producing rounded students aware of their social responsibilities.

The big picture

Over recent years, the form tutor role has undergone another sea change, with the emphasis moving away from administrative routines towards academic and social target setting. As the idea of 'assessment for learning' has become central to school and student progress, the form tutor has been seen as key to successfully nurturing this idea. Uniquely of all teachers, the form tutor has the ability to overview a student's progress across all subjects, and to work with that student to set appropriate and achievable targets. So, as a form tutor you will play a key part in how your tutor group see themselves as learners, and you will have the ability to positively shape their development as students.

Perspectives

For a wider perspective it is useful to see how various people in education view the role. Looking at differing opinions will help you develop your tutoring skills while keeping a weather eye on the range of expectations of you. All form tutors will have a line manager to offer support and advice, but the exciting aspect of the role is that you can develop it to suit your own personal ideas and approaches.

Experienced teachers

Experienced teachers' views of form tutoring seem to fall into two distinct camps. The first, and largest, is the group that sees it as a necessary evil that gets in the way of their 'real' task – to deliver a subject. This may actually be a response to the fact that training and support needs are not being met and so the role is not given status. This book will help address those issues. The second, smaller group is of people who often make a career within the pastoral system. They embrace the role and see it as vital.

You will be part of a year team made up of a mix of the two points of view, the biggest issue being your delivery of tutorial/PSHE lessons. As form tutor you will be asked to deliver a range of pastoral topics well outside your comfort zone and subject specialism.

There is one constant though: those teachers who grudgingly undertake a form tutor's role will expect instant support from you if one of your tutees causes problems in their lessons!

Senior management

Form tutors come under a lot of pressure to 'do a good job'. As one senior manager, an experienced deputy head, summed it up:

'The tutor has to tread the line between supporting a student and following the school rules. Explanation and reinforcement of key rules and routines must be a primary responsibility; a good form tutor helps the smooth running of the school by keeping on top of student appearance and behaviour. In addition, tutors should use data to get a good view of a student's academic ability.'

While different senior managers will have slightly different views, this is a good starting point for you to think about how you can develop your own tutoring persona.

Head of year

One step down from SMT will be your daily line manager, usually your head of year. He or she will keep you briefed about key student issues and will provide support for your tutorial activities. Heads of year in one school outlined key aspects of the role as follows.

A good form tutor will:

- Establish key school routines
- Form positive relationships with tutees
- Quickly follow up absences
- Keep good records of interaction with parents/carers
- Set good targets
- Support and inform colleagues over matters of discipline
- Deliver PSHE programmes well
- Be able to act as part of a year team

Year heads tend to a more 'nuts and bolts' view of the role than the more strategic view of senior management. How you deal with the two expectations is important as you develop as a tutor.

Students

The most critical viewpoint! When students were asked the question, 'What do you want from your form tutor?' their main responses were:

- Someone who listens and helps me when I fall out with friends or have trouble with other teachers
- Is friendly and approachable
- Takes an interest in me
- Knows what they are doing (!)

A common reaction from upper school students was that a good form tutor 'doesn't hassle us with tutorial stuff' but 'helps with GCSE work'. This type of response can open up useful dialogue with your students, but also signposts ways in which you can support them. For example, you may want to give over some time to whole-class 'brainstorming' of study issues.

Student questionnaires can be very helpful in informing your role as a form tutor.

Parents

The form tutor is often the first 'port of call' for parents/guardians who are feeling fairly fraught about things. It is important to see your job from their perspective. A parent will seek quick contact for a range of reasons and it is easy to overlook the importance of returning calls promptly. Parents expect form tutors to:

- Listen
- Take an effective role in sorting out problems, often seeing you as a 'go between' with colleagues
- Act on their child's behalf, (sometimes even if school rules and procedures suggest otherwise)
- Make their child feel happy and settled

Pages 45-54 look in more detail at working with parents and carers.

Ofsted

The Ofsted view is best gleaned from a trawl through their various publications. Their *'Handbook for Inspecting Secondary Schools'* throws light on the areas they are concerned about. Section 6 is titled 'How well are students cared for, guided and supported?' These three key areas are ones you should aim to focus on in your form tutor role:

- Care
- Guidance
- Support

This pocketbook will help you to build your skills in these areas.

A human face

The key to effective and satisfying form tutoring is to be aware of the views and expectations outlined on the previous pages, and to **develop the job according to your own particular personality and ideas**. Of all teaching jobs, form tutoring is the one where you can let more of your real personality shine through – if you have a form for five years, it is very difficult to keep up an act for so long!

As such, it is a positive and energising experience: you will see the rewards as the students in your tutor group are gently shaped and encouraged by how you deal with them, within the framework of whole-school pastoral policies. Remember, you will be the 'human face' of rules and regulations! You will also be a role model for those students, so be sure that any of your personality that might rub off on them is positive!

The following profiles might provide food for thought!

The Stalinist

- Enforces rigorous discipline and instils the fear of God. Routines are drilled into students. Their form is always the one that marches in single file to assembly, is able to wait in a fire-drill line in silence, and whose day books are always signed

- Regularly has four or five tutees in detention for such heinous crimes as day book being signed one day late, or tie not knotted correctly

- Blissfully unaware that they displace bad behaviour all around the school, as free from his or her baleful glare the form runs riot with all teachers not cast in the same mould

The ditherer

- Misplaces register, paperwork and, occasionally, members of the form

- Frequently late to registration, often when there is a drive for student punctuality. Never bothers to check up on the school rules they are meant to be enforcing

- Their class love them, and such love breeds imitation – their students are often late, disorganised and without a shred of malice

Best friend

- Knows all the latest stuff – which mobile phone to have, current bands, fashion, students' buzzwords
- Chats to the form as if they were younger brothers and sisters. Proud of ability to build relationships with tutees. If female, wears dangly earrings; if male, fashionably scruffy
- Will discipline tutees with knowing smiles and absolutely no impact

Mr/Ms contractual obligation

- Knows what a form tutor has to do as a legal minimum and sticks to it
- Once register is called will read paper or plan lessons while tutees get on with whatever they like
- Form notices are simply stuck to the wall without comment
- Treats form members as personal slaves, using them to tidy up classroom/sort subject resources, etc
- Goes a funny colour when asked to deliver pastoral work, then does so via a 'read sheet and write answers' methodology

The campaigner

- Urges form to discuss 'issues' ranging from animal experiments to the role of women/men
- Will encourage students to put together a petition at the drop of a hat
- Wears at least one piece of jewellery/adornment linked to a cause
- Stridently makes form volunteer to collect charity/non-uniform money or build the biggest harvest box
- Often so involved in stoking the fires of debate that such things as uniform checks, and even taking the register, sometimes pass them by

You!

And then there's you!

- Interested in what the students are doing socially, but slightly distanced from them
- Wise enough to bend the rules, without breaking them in the students' favour
- A good listener and a fair disciplinarian
- Approachable, without being a substitute elder sibling
- Encouraging students in their successes, academic and pastoral
- Cultivator of a positive atmosphere for growing up

A positive and supportive guide to help them as they move through their school career and the various challenges of 'being a pupil'.

Notes

What Do They Want from Me?

 Routines and Admin ◀

 Working with Parents and Carers

 Pastoral and Social Development

 Effective Target Setting

 Ideas for Tutorials

 Professional Development

Routines and Admin

Help and support

In your capacity as form tutor you will be working with a number of **colleagues** who can support you in what you do and give advice and guidance over policies and procedures.

You will also need to deal with a range of regular **tasks** efficiently and quickly. This chapter is aimed at outlining who there is in a school to help and support you, and to highlight important routines and admin, with ideas on how to set up strategies to aid your work.

Key people

Titles will vary slightly from school to school, as will their precise areas of support, but broadly speaking, these are the people who can support you:

- **Head of year**. Often known as **year co-ordinator**, this is the teacher responsible for all tutors on your year team. He/she will brief you about your form, and will provide resources if you have to deliver aspects of a pastoral programme. Heads of year will also have clear routines and recording methods for a range of issues, including contacting parents

- **Other tutors** in the school and **your year team**. Don't overlook the obvious – these colleagues are doing the same job as you and will be useful sources of support and ideas

- **School counsellor**. Some schools now have trained counselling staff available to support students over confidential issues. They will be able to give you guidance on a number of matters

Key people (cont'd)

- **Child protection officer**. This is usually a senior member of staff and, though the title varies from school to school, the role is the same. Their job is to deal with disclosures of abuse and other such problems. Your school will inform you of the precise nature of their role, and also the steps to take if a student discloses information to you. It is essential to find out exactly what constitutes a matter referable to the CPO as these are potentially very serious issues. Both your head of year and CPO should brief you on confidentiality issues in such cases

When in doubt refer a matter to the child protection officer.

Key people (cont'd)

- **Office staff**. As a busy form tutor you will find the office staff an essential source of support. They will deal with a host of paperwork on your behalf, and are often the first people to deal with irate parents/carers intent on arguing with you!

Make an effort to cultivate your office staff – flowers or chocolates at Christmas, for example, and regular 'thank yous' remind them that they are appreciated. Their workload is heavy, and their support for you can make a crucial difference to how you manage your own workload.

Registration time

It may well be that you find yourself in a school that has moved a lot of the administrative side of the job away from you to admin staff. On the other hand, you may work in a school with a more traditional view of a form tutor's duties. Whatever the systems and support, a typical registration period will go like this:

- You will take your register
- Students will give you a variety of notes about past or future absences
- Whole-school notices will be read out, and old notices re-read out for reinforcement
- You will keep a weather eye on uniform
- Some students will come to you for resources they have forgotten, like pens
- There will be some sort of disagreement to sort out

If you are lucky, you may have as long as fifteen minutes to organise all of the above.

Registers

Taking the register is a main area of change for schools. Many now have electronic registers and you need to familiarise yourself with the different codes used to record reasons for student absence. Some schools have admin staff to input some of the codes, but always check to see which ones *you* are expected to enter. Other schools still have paper registers; you may even be expected to transcribe these annually.

The register is a legal document and there is a legal requirement to track absences, so be sure you know exactly what your school wants you to do. You also need to discuss this with your tutees, as students are often unaware of how important the register is, or its legal status as a document that can be quoted in a court of law. This will allow some useful discussion of the importance of providing notes for absence, and the importance of attendance!

Organising the paperwork

Many schools now have good support systems for form tutors, and the workforce remodelling agreement means you are unlikely to have to investigate student absences. However, you may well have to deal with absence notes. You should check with your line manager about where to hand the various notes you receive; you may need to set up an effective filing system of your own. The simplest is to keep two different colour folders, one for absence notes, and one for any other communications from home.

Keeping track by initialling and dating letters when you are given them makes a useful archive for discussing issues with both students and parents. For example, if a student regularly hands notes in late, it is helpful to be able to show them a run of their notes with the dates on which you received them.

Setting the tone

Form tutors have the ability to set the student mood for the day. A cheerful and positive morning registration will have a 'knock on' effect in the following lessons. The knack is to set up good routines and behaviour without creating conflict.

It is useful to set out your stall from 'day one' of taking on a form. You could ask the class to answer the register in a certain way, *'Yes Sir/Miss'* for example to set the tone, and then couple it with the reinforcement of a school rule (such as 'coats off'). It is also helpful to discuss expectations with the class. These can be usefully made into a display by the students to have on the wall as a constant reminder of how they are to behave in registration, eg:

- Headwear off
- Sit in your chair
- No talking
- Day books out for checking

Setting the tone

- Headwear off!

- No talking

- Sit in your chair

- Day books out for checking

School rules

Humour is a very positive tool for a form tutor to employ. Equipment and jewellery checks can be more effective if carried out with humour,

'How can you hold your head up with those earrings? Please take them off!'

or,

'I didn't realise orange was the new school bag colour!'

Always follow up any comments like these with the mantra, *'You know the school rules'*. This way you constantly reinforce why you are doing something, and eventually students will see not to take such reproofs personally, especially if you have the school rules clearly on display.

Confiscation

For your part, be aware of the exact steps to take when personal items are confiscated from students, and get the students to make a flow chart for display, eg:

1. State school rule.
2. Confiscation by tutor and note in day book.
3. Tutor puts items in envelope and takes to office.
4. Student may retrieve at end of week.

By keeping such school rules in plain sight and referring to them regularly, you can show the students that it is nothing personal, just you doing your job – *and they theirs by following the school procedures!*

Display space

It is a good idea to earmark some form room space specifically as a display zone for your tutees. This will be a useful area not only to show key aspects of school rules, but also for student-made current affairs information. A space like this helps students feel a sense of ownership of the room. Their display zone can also be used to support study skills and revision, with them producing and pinning up memory aids such as revision cards, brainstorm diagrams and mnemonics. There are some suggestions for these in the 'Ideas for Tutorials' section.

Notices and activities

It is helpful if you can also have a form notice-board for messages. This allows the students to see, rather than just hear, bulletins etc. It also discourages dependence on you as the 'notice-giver' by prompting students to be responsible for finding out new information themselves.

Set up sections to include information about fire drills, key term dates, school clubs and sporting fixtures. Involve students in putting up new notices and taking down out-of-date ones (you could have a notice-board monitor rota for this) to encourage them to look at the board themselves.

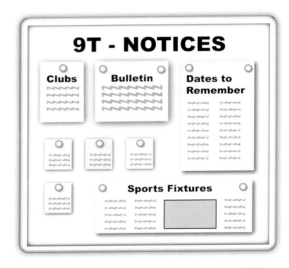

The day book

All form tutors quickly come across the day book in one of its guises – it is sometimes called a contact book, or it may be the homework diary. It is a key component in the management of your form. In it, students will write down their homework and important messages; parents will sometimes use the book to write notes to you; other teachers will put notes in it about students (both praise and criticism).

You will be expected to sign these books once a week, as will the parents. If used properly, they will give you a good 'across the board' snapshot of how your tutees are doing and are valuable tools for communicating with parents. Signing is very time-intensive. *It may be easier to allocate a particular day of the week for it.* The alternative is to sign five or six each day, rather than the whole class's at once.

Drill yourself to walk around your form room, casually accessing the books on a regular basis. Get the students used to the fact that you expect to peruse their books to see how they are doing. This will also help you interact with them and get to know them better.

Uniform

As a form tutor you will be the school's frontline for school uniform rules enforcement. This can be done informally on a daily basis by Your Good Self, but often will be asked for by an announcement from SMT. In that case you need to prepare yourself for the dreaded **uniform check**.

Be prepared to learn about such exotica as 'box pleat skirts' and appropriate tie lengths. Develop advanced haggling skills as to what exactly constitutes a tucked in shirt, or appropriate skirt length. Humour helps with such weighty issues:

'Hoody down please, it's not likely to rain inside the classroom.'

Whole-school requirements

In addition to daily requirements, there are a number of weekly and half-termly or termly responsibilities for a form tutor. These include setting up representative groups to link your form to whole-school procedures, as well as instituting a form committee to share the workload with you and give the students a degree of independence.

- **Class committees**. Usually reviewed termly, though half-termly can get more students involved. Typically, these will include election or appointment of students to various roles such as form captain, sports captain, charity officer, and librarian
- **School council reps/meetings**. Usually for the whole year – a couple of students to represent the form at whole-year council meetings. It's a good idea to give time every fortnight or so for students to air their views for the representatives to take to the full meeting

You can help the form establish a sense of identity, and a feeling of being part of wider school activities by raising the profile of class committees and school council representation. So make sure that you 'talk the roles up'.

Voting, committees and councils

You can set up class committees and councils in different ways:

- Secret ballot, where you prepare voting papers and have a cardboard ballot box for students to use. The front of the form room can have a voting table, discreetly shielded from the rest of the form where each student walks up to mark their paper
- Heads down, thumbs up voting, where students rest their heads on their arms, eyes closed, and as you read out each candidate's name they vote by raising their thumb. You tally the votes on the board
- Drawing lots with student names on
- You simply appoint students into roles

It is useful to get the students used to some sort of voting system as it helps build a sense of teamwork. Keep an eye on the rotation of responsibilities – try to ensure everyone gets some sort of responsibility over the course of the school year.

Elections

If you want to really 'go to town'
you could set up formal elections,
where candidates are nominated
and then give a short speech to the
form outlining why they deserve to
be elected. Alternatively, each
candidate could be encouraged to
produce a short 'manifesto' of ideas
at home to give to the form.

Thought for the week

Usually weekly, but sometimes daily, and aimed at fulfilling the 'whole-school act of worship' requirement, your school may require you to deliver a 'thought'. Try some different approaches:

- Booklet-making based on the theme
- A regular discussion registration
- A homework task where students have to bring in things linked to the 'thought for the week' topic
- A moment of quiet reflection, where you give a couple of minutes of registration time to contemplation of the ideas
- Most schools will give you the thought for the week, but you can often find your own way of linking it to issues in the news, moral dilemmas or citizenship content to encourage your tutor group to explore 'the thought' more deeply
- You could set up an imaginary family and discuss with the form how the family would react to each particular issue raised by the thought for the week. This helps to link the issues together as the form see how different people can respond to different (or the same) situations

Report writing

In recent years there has been a major change to the responsibilities of form tutors regarding reports. Reports should now be collated and checked by administrative staff, rather than tutors. Similarly, attendance statistics needed for the reports are no longer generated by you poring over your register, but are produced centrally.

What remains the same is that you will be provided with the completed subject reports to read and to add to. Check exactly what you are being invited to comment on: some schools will want you to write a summary overview of the report across all the subjects; others will want you to comment only on pastoral matters, including use of form time and attendance.

The praise sandwich

If invited to overview the report, always aim to be mostly positive – the 'praise sandwich' is a good approach:

'Paul has achieved good exam results in geography, which is pleasing. He should look to focus more on his French work. Paul's effort grade for P.E. is very pleasing.'

The advice is placed between two praise points.

If only commenting on pastoral matters, useful positive phrases include:

'...has a stable friendship base in the form.'
'...takes an active part in tutorial work.'
'...has settled well to the new year.'
'...readily gives an opinion during form discussions.'

What Do They Want from Me?

 Routines and Admin

 Working with Parents and Carers ◀

 Pastoral and Social Development

 Effective Target Setting

 Ideas for Tutorials

 Professional Development

Working with Parents and Carers

Effective relationships

As a form tutor you will be an important point of contact for parents/carers who see you as the public face of the school. A key point to remember about the relationship you build with them over the years: *it is a reciprocal one*. You can support them and they will support you with discipline, prompt return of reply slips, and regular signing of day books, etc. And remember, they like to hear about positive things as well as negative, so:

DON'T CONTACT PARENTS/CARERS **JUST** WHEN THERE IS A PROBLEM

Try, also, to have some contact beyond tutor evenings etc., at least once a term. It may be something as simple as a friendly note in the day book, or a quick phone call to say everything is going well. This will help put a personal face to a sometimes impersonal school service.

Building a friendly atmosphere

You may well have completely different feelings about school than some of the parents or carers you deal with. It is worth remembering that whereas for most teachers school was a happy experience which had value, this is not necessarily the case for all adults. For some, school may be seen as an unfriendly and threatening place. It is up to you, as a form tutor, to be sensitive to this and take steps to put parents and carers at their ease, not only when they come in to see you, but also in how you deal with their telephone enquiries.

Simple phrases, especially ones that invite them to offer solutions, work best:

'How can I help you?'
'What would you like me to do?'

Body language

If possible, as part of your professional development, ask for some training on reading and using body language. At the very least read around the subject, so that when you meet with parents/carers you can spot danger signs and avoid creating a hostile atmosphere by the subconscious signals you are sending out.

- Leaning towards parents as they raise points shows interest, but can also be seen as aggressive if you are speaking
- Try to give parents a clear view past you so that they don't feel boxed in – standing or sitting slightly to one side helps
- Avoid interrupting, even if you really disagree with what they say
- Echo words and phrases the parent/carer uses
- Mirror their body language. When they start copying yours, they are onside
- If the situation becomes openly hostile, remove yourself from the room to allow things to calm down

Building bridges

There are many ways to get parents/carers onside:

- If parents/carers send you a note, make sure you acknowledge receipt with a 'thanks' in the day book, or on the note returned to parents via the student
- Return phone calls on the day you get them
- Listen to parents/carers – don't butt in or make it obvious that you think they are wrong. Sometimes they need to vent before you can work on the problem
- Make notes of points parents/carers raise and get them to agree that the notes cover the issues discussed. (Useful as a point of reference and matter of record for the future, as well as showing that you are taking in what is being said)

In all things be prompt and appear to be interested.

One golden rule

If you tell a parent or carer you will get back to them at a certain date, make sure you do it, *even if there is nothing to report beyond what you last spoke about*. This gives them the security of knowing that you remember them and care about their offspring.

Failure to fulfil the contact promise – even if done with good intentions – will cause parents to think that you don't care or, even worse, have forgotten the issues.

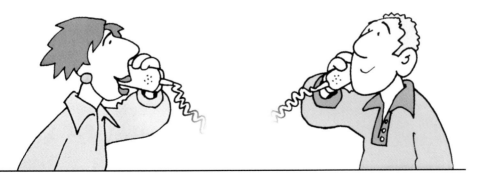

Custody and care

You need to be very careful and make sure that you know who in your form lives with whom. Students may be sensitive, for instance, about an absent parent being assumed to be in the parental home. Similarly, you need to know who is not with parents but may be looked after in care or with foster parents, etc. With this information you can avoid upsetting a student unknowingly. Your line manager will support you in building your knowledge about your form. To help yourself, keep a **confidential** list.

Divorce/separation

You may have to deal with fairly fraught parental situations, typically where parents have separated and have a difficult relationship with each other. You can support a student in this very difficult situation.

- If reports go out, make sure the office is aware of which parent(s)/guardian(s) get reports and when
- Be sure you know of any court arrangements about access and keep an unobtrusive watch on how this affects the student at school. Does behaviour or work fall away when student has access to the estranged parent?
- Keep colleagues advised if a student is staying with an estranged parent as part of access, as they will often leave schoolbooks, etc. accidentally where they have stayed for the weekend. Similar for uniform issues
- Chat with the student about their work/social life and open up an opportunity for them to talk about what is going on

Making a difference

Building good relationships with parents is a key way to help students achieve their best at school. This is why the form tutor's job is so important. Always *listen* to parents' views – *whatever you think about the truth of the matter* – and be prepared to acknowledge their viewpoints. Inviting the parents to offer a solution is a very powerful way of getting them to think through the problem in hand. It will help open up a dialogue and gives them an input as to what steps are taken next.

Creating a good impression

By building a good relationship with parents and carers you will also be helping the school's reputation in the wider community. It is important to remember that the image you convey, in those brief meetings with parents, is the image that the parent will take away of the school. So a 30 minute meeting with a parent/carer will have a disproportionate effect on them. Preparation is the key:

- Check that you have the right pupil in mind! Use class photos to double-check
- Read any file held on the pupil before meeting the parents
- Tidy up your appearance
- Greet the parents with a smile and a simple opening phrase such as *'What can I do for you?'*

If you have no time to prepare, then the first and last bullet points are essential!

What Do
They Want
from Me?

 Routines
and Admin

 Working with
Parents and
Carers

 Pastoral
and Social
Development

 Effective
Target
Setting

 Ideas for
Tutorials

 Professional
Development

Pastoral
and Social
Development

Team-building

One of the most enjoyable aspects of form tutoring is taking on a new tutor group and shaping them into a collection of individuals who have independence yet team characteristics. You really can be a major influence over a student's development as a person and, remember, for some of the form you may well be the only regular fixed adult dealing with them as they grow up.

The skill is to foster a group ethos while allowing students to retain their individuality. You should aim to cultivate an atmosphere that is socially diverse, but respectful of difference, one where students can have their own viewpoints about the world, while also respecting others'.

A good form is a collection of individuals who can pull together as a team. The following pages should help you build your team toward this end.

Finding out about your form

When you take over a form there is one important point to keep checking:
Have I spoken to each member of my form over the past week?
This is essential if you are to begin to develop relationships with your tutees.

- Drill yourself to meet your tutor group as they arrive; say *'Hello'*
- Move around your form room and chat
- Say *'Hi!'* to members of your form when you see them around school
- Talk to the students to find out 'what makes them tick'
- Find out what their hobbies are, and get them to bring in things linked to their interests to show you and the rest of the group

If you take an interest in what they do and who they are, they begin to see you as *theirs*.

Taking over a form

Taking over someone else's form can be quite a challenge – you may be following in the footsteps of a favourite teacher, or may be expected to 'sort out' a form where tutoring was not a strength of your predecessor.

It is useful to adopt a frank 'bygones are bygones' approach. Tell the form that this is an entirely fresh start, and nothing from the past – good or bad – will influence your relationship with them. This gives everyone the chance to move forward together.

Invite the students in your form to tell you something about themselves when you first meet. The simplest way is to go down the register, as this also helps put faces to names. Use the birthday/likes checklist below as a quick way of making inroads.

Name	Birthday	Likes	Dislikes
Jo Green	15/May	Cats, music	Snow

When a colleague gave each of his new tutor group a birthday card and issued personalised Christmas cards en masse, the effect on morale was enormous.

Trips

Look to set up a whole-form social event that will help foster group identity. The following venues have been used to good effect by experienced colleagues, following a class vote as to which location would be best!

- Ice skating
- Ten-pin bowling
- Pantomime/theatre trip

As you get to know your students, you will find that extra-curricular interaction and knowledge will deepen your relationship with the class. You could then get students to research and plan a trip for the form or, perhaps, look to see if there are any residential trip opportunities. It may even be that your school would welcome such an 'enrichment' idea for the whole year group.

The 'Trips and Visits Pocketbook' has helpful details on planning, organising and running events like these.

Whole-school events

Whole-school events such as assembly and sports day can also foster form unity. It may well be that your form has to deliver an assembly to their peers. This is a good chance for you to support your students as they work together. Try to ensure that every student has something to do, even if it only involves standing at the back of the stage.

Sports days help build form spirit, but don't just concentrate on the athletes. Create a cheerleading-type support team with the non-athletes in the form. Use some tutor-time to get students making banners and thinking up suitable chants to encourage their classmates.

Team-building checklist

As you develop your tutoring role keep this list in mind. You may look at some things on the list as monthly checkpoints, and others as termly.

- ◯ Have I checked that each form member is doing well in their lessons?
- ◯ Have I organised a form trip this term?
- ◯ Have I communicated with all parents – even just a quick note in a day book?
- ◯ Have I sat and chatted with each friendship group during tutor time?
- ◯ If I have disciplined a form member, have I built a friendly bridge back towards them?
- ◯ Do I regularly meet and greet the form at the door?
- ◯ Have I praised the whole form regularly?
- ◯ Do I know each form member's likes and dislikes?
- ◯ Which form members have siblings?
- ◯ Which form members have pets?
- ◯ Have I followed up 'X's request/problem?

PSHE as a resource

You will get a great deal of support, not only from your line manager, but also from your school's PSHE programme. Although you may not be part of the team delivering this pastoral programme, your students will be learning useful strategies for how to deal with social issues, such as falling out with friends, bullying, managing arguments, and a host of other matters.

You should familiarise yourself with what pastoral programmes are being delivered to your tutees. This will let you pick up and develop topics during tutor time.

Look to adopt particular approaches from the PSHE programme. For example, often there is an emphasis on talking through problems; use this approach with your students in their contact with you.

Each school will have a slightly different ethos regarding PSHE work, so get a feel for how your school wants you to work.

Role-play

You can get students to work through difficulties by using role-play. Assign emotions or points of view to *things* rather than people. For example, set up an 'angry' table and a 'calm' table. Sit the students at each table and get them to talk through a problem using the table's assigned point of view. Also, try role-play using other opposites – 'loud' and 'quiet' solutions, for instance.

Character cards also work well, as students are guided to play out the problem from the perspective of someone else. This simple character card is useful, because it incorporates an element of change:

Joe

You are frustrated rather than angry.

You believe you are right and state your point of view.

You are able to listen to others.

You have admitted being wrong in previous arguments.

Character sheets

Quiet, non-active role-plays are also very positive in letting students work problems and issues through. They can help more reticent members of the form to explore issues.

One simple idea is to get each student to use a character sheet on which they write down how that character would deal with the particular problem. This can then be used to generate class discussion as to whose character reacts best in the situation. Use the responses to outline an 'ideal' response to model to your students.

Discipline

Sometimes you will need to discipline a member of your form. It is important to be clear as to the focus and limited nature of the discipline, so that a student in your form does not feel they cannot access you for help at a later date.

Cultivate a reputation of not bearing grudges; try not to carry over feelings of ill will towards more difficult members of the form.

One important step towards this is engaging with the student around school, and particularly the day after the discipline, in a friendly and positive way, perhaps highlighting something that went well elsewhere in the student's school day.

Managing difficult students

Dealing with difficult students in your form is not easy! Your line manager will help, but there are a number of strategies you can try. A difficult student will often end up on some sort of official report that you have to check, and this needs careful handling as well.

Always greet the student with a smile and engage in direct conversation with them that is not linked to school. Simply asking them how their evening went can be useful.

Try to check the student report privately, and keep the student close to you. This may involve moving to a quiet part of the room, or even temporarily standing outside the room (keep the door open). You are aiming to cultivate a personal one-to-one feel for the student (as well as taking away any possible 'playing to the gallery'). Discuss with them how they think their behaviour is impacting on the form, and look to offer support, eg *'If you feel yourself getting wound up, just go out of the room – no need to ask permission'*.

Behaviour log

One simple approach that works well is to get the student to review each day
for you on a formal written questionnaire. The act of writing will encourage them to
reflect on what has happened during the day, and allow you to keep a written archive
of how the student progresses through the time they are in trouble. This short
questionnaire has proved very effective:

What went well for you
today, and why?

What didn't go so well,
and why?

What can you do differently
tomorrow to make things go better?

Positive behaviour management

As a form tutor you will often feel as if you are between a rock and a hard place. Staff will expect you to support their disciplining your students, while students will look to you for support over those same measures. It is important to strike a balance between being accessible to students and supporting colleagues.

One method is to avoid the word 'detention' when you keep a student behind on a colleague's behalf. Instead, cultivate the culture of this being 'counselling time' or 'mentoring time'. Although the effect is the same as a detention for the student (ie they are kept back), the outcome will be more positive. This approach also lets you explore issues with the student and helps them build bridges back towards appropriate relationships with their teachers. *'How are you going to fix this?'* is a very powerful question to ask the student in these sessions.

Another strategy is to make the student aware that you know they are having problems by greeting them with a, *'Morning Pete, what's going on in Maths?'* This will allow the student to talk about the problem if they want to, while showing them you are aware of their 'difficulties'.

Rewards

Developing an 'in-house' rewards system for your form will also help your discipline. You could set up 'good comments' or 'smiley faces' on a chart of the form that everyone can see, with rewards for every 10 good comments or faces. (Chocolates and sweets are rarely seen as a bad thing!)

Alternatively, you could put the form into reward teams and allocate good comments to the teams to give positive behaviour a competitive edge. You could ask the class to set out exactly what they need to do in tutor time and around school to gain rewards.

Don't forget, positive rewards often stop bad behaviour from developing.

Tutoring challenges

There is a key phrase to continually bring before your form that will help them learn how to deal with arguments:

> *'Only react to what you heard and saw, not to what someone told you or claimed they saw themselves'*

This will help the students (and you!) deal with the three horsemen of 'Rumour', 'Stirrer' and 'Liar.' Repeat the phrase often to drive the message home.

'Did you actually see/hear what upset you?' is a very useful starting point when talking one-to-one with a student. It will echo the whole class point, but allow you to develop a helpful dialogue with the tutee.

Handling arguments

Dealing with arguments among students is not easy. One helpful measure is to get all the students involved to write down their view of things. Not only does this give them time to reflect, it also gives you a record to go on when trying to heal rifts, and when dealing with concerned parents/carers.

- Try to let each student have their say, however at odds it is with the facts
- Give students time and space to write their version of events down
- Indicate to parents on the day of the problem that you are dealing with it. This will prevent anxious phone calls
- Remember that what you see as trivial things are magnified in importance from the perspective of a child

Friendship problems

Friendship breakdown is a common problem that you need to manage.
Generally, in Year 7 classes these happen at a bewilderingly fast rate and are repaired just as quickly. Further on up the school, friendship splits can be more serious and harder to heal, so you need to counsel your students about ways of dealing with friendship breakdowns, and how best to act if they are irretrievable. Before you intervene, keep these two points in mind

- Sometimes you need do no more than provide a listening ear or tell students to wait until after the weekend before you deal with their problems. You may well find that all is well again come Monday

- Usually friendships are repaired by the students, but you need to keep an unobtrusive eye on things to make sure there is no genuine isolation or deeper problems

Working through friendship breakdowns

If you choose to get involved, a useful approach is to get all the students involved to sit down together with you and talk the problem through. Give students a chance to formulate their own bridge-building. Ask them, *'What are you going to do to deal with this problem?'*

If emotions are running high, use shuttle diplomacy. See each party separately and get them to jot down their points of difference. Then bring them together once tempers have cooled. By this point you should have a clearer picture of what went on, as well as an idea of how to move the students forward.

It is also useful, before you talk to the main protagonists, to quietly seek out other students and get their perspective on what is going on.

Supporting and listening

When dealing with problems, aim to **support and listen**. This can be very difficult to do if you are aiming to enforce discipline, but a good form tutor will try always to listen to what their students say, even if disagreeing with their point of view. This attitude will help you build a relationship with the student even as you are sanctioning them. Use phrases that help a student work through an issue:

'What do you want to do about this?'
'How can I help you here?'
'How can you get yourself out of this problem?'
'Why did that happen?'
'What will you do differently next time this happens?'

But sometimes it is perfectly valid to say, *'You've had your say, but this is what I think...'*

Managing student workload

To support your students' academic development you will need to monitor workload and homework. Some students find these matters especially difficult to cope with. Try to make sure you chat to all members of the tutor group about their work to pick up on any problems. Help them plan a simple homework timetable and keep a copy yourself. When you see the student at daily registration, get them to tick off what they have done from the plan.

In your capacity as tutor, you can also help by finding out various work deadlines and displaying them on the notice-board. Reinforce this weeks before the actual deadline by raising it as a whole-class discussion point in tutor time.

Keeping pupils on track

One potentially serious academic problem will begin to surface as students go through the school: some students will positively dislike a range of subjects and will need strategies to keep them on track and out of trouble.

Look for signs of trouble, and **talk to the student(s) concerned**. Signs of trouble will include notes from teachers in the day book, your tutee telling you more than once they have forgotten books for a particular lesson, or sudden, odd patterns of absence (as a way of avoiding a subject). Intervene early, and gently.

- Ask to look at the student's books and have a general chat about how they are doing across all subjects
- Be open about suspicions as to absences
- Talk to the subject teacher(s) involved to see if there is a real problem, or whether the student is imagining a range of faults that don't exist

Bullying

All schools will have a clear bullying policy, with advice about what steps to take if bullying is suspected. Some schools may well not involve form tutors in the process at all, preferring heads of year and trained counsellors to deal with the students involved. Be sure you are aware of how your school expects you to deal with bullying before you act.

Some general approaches can be useful. For example, use tutor time to discuss 'What makes a bully?' and 'What things count as bullying?' Also challenge the students with role-plays and discussions to look at *reasons for and solutions to* bullying.

Look at how your school PSHE and Citizenship programmes deal with the problem, and take advice. The *Stop Bullying Pocketbook* (see page 109) has a range of helpful suggestions.

Bereavement

It is worth asking to go on a bereavement course as part of your professional development. Few of us are equipped to know how best to respond to a death, for instance of someone in our form, or of a close family member of one of our tutees. You are not expected to cope alone. Such a serious matter will be dealt with by your line manager or a member of the leadership team. You can expect support from them.

It is best to follow professional counselling advice rather than trying to improvise. Generally, however, you will need to give a bereaved student time and space to deal with their emotions. Make them aware that they can access you at any time during the school day. Alert your colleagues, and give the student a simple note to show to their teacher if they want to leave a lesson to find you, eg *'X is very upset today, please let him/her come to see me during a lesson. Thanks.'*

Talking about bereavement is a positive way of coping with grief. Just by listening you can help.

Bereavement

If the student is to be away, reassure them that you will sort out any work that might be missed. Photocopy work for them if you can, as they will not be able to catch up with pages of work from each subject. Go out of your way to liaise with the student's school friends, even if they are not in your form. This kind of practical help is valuable.

Managing bereavement is a specialist skill. You may be able to access professional support from outside agencies or the school counsellor. See page 109 for suggested further reading.

Boyfriends/girlfriends

As your tutor group moves through the school, boyfriends and girlfriends will begin to loom larger in students' lives, and you may well find yourself counselling tutees who are emotionally upset over this issue for the first time.

- Buy a box of tissues!
- Talk to the student with one of their friends to give support
- Seek the student out around the school to keep a friendly eye on them
- Ask a friend of the student to chat to them and then report back to you
- Make sure there is no underlying serious issue like pregnancy, or boys about to fight over a girl – or vice versa!

Guiding them at this stage will help show them how to deal with similarly emotive issues as adults.

Getting pupils to talk

If one of your students seems upset or out of sorts, ask this question:

'Is it home, school, or personal?'
Follow up with, *'Do you want me to help?'*

This allows you to know generally what is upsetting them, and will let you gently follow up at a later date.

It is as important just to listen to students when they tell you their problems, as it is to offer advice. If you listen carefully, you will see that many students already have an idea of how to deal with the matter, and simply want you to hear or approve of what they intend to do.

Making time for your tutees

As you build a relationship with your form, you need to balance the need *they* will have to seek you out for support with the need *you* have to take breaks and deliver your lessons. Some possible solutions:

- Have a 'talking space' in your room where students can quietly access you in form time/registration
- Cultivate the culture of the 'corridor chat', where you take the student(s) into the corridor to talk with them (while keeping a careful eye on the rest of the form left in the room)
- Set up fixed access time, for example a couple of break times or one half of lunch on a given day

But be flexible: sometimes a student will have an urgent reason to access you outside the times you have set up. Allow this and students will learn only to do it over genuinely urgent issues.

Form self-assessment guide

You can use this self-assessment guide with your form at various points in the year to see how they are doing as a unit, and to highlight areas you, their form tutor, need to concentrate on.

I feel happy in the form.	1	2	3	4	5
I feel that my views are listened to in form time.	1	2	3	4	5
I think form time is well used.	1	2	3	4	5
I want to help out on the form committee.	1	2	3	4	5
We discuss important issues in form time.	1	2	3	4	5
We have a sense of the form being a team.	1	2	3	4	5
We support one another around the school.	1	2	3	4	5
I find my form tutor helpful.	1	2	3	4	5

Use the results to generate discussion and to shape how you work with your form.

Referrals and confidentiality

When dealing with student problems, it is crucial to be absolutely upfront with the student that you can never promise to keep a secret; you cannot offer confidentiality if you deem the issue a serious one.

If you have any doubt about the best course of action to take once you have chatted with a student, or the degree of seriousness of the matter raised, refer it to your line manager immediately. Also, keep your line manager up to date about any issues you are dealing with so that they can support you.

If a student discloses abuse to you, it is very important to refer this IMMEDIATELY to the appropriate member of staff, writing down exactly what was said to you.

In a similar vein, issues linked to self-abuse, depression and mental health need to be referred to the appropriate professionals. You are not expected to have to deal with such issues, and sometimes a 'helpful amateur' approach can actually make the situation worse.

Effective Target Setting

Why set targets?

Targets are central to assessment for learning, whereby the student is put at the centre of the assessment process and given the ideas and assessment vocabulary to monitor and develop their own learning. As a form tutor, you are crucial to the success of this key process.

Data types

Form tutors are given a wide range of data to inform their work with tutees. Your line manager will explain and support your use of such data.

Depending on your school, you may get CAT scores, VR scores, national curriculum levels, quartile grade ranges, information from YELLIS, and ALIS grading, to list but a few. The one thing they have in common is that they will all be set up to give a broad indication of a student's ability. You need to avoid the 'reducing a student to a number' type analysis, and always keep a firm eye on the human angle.

As form tutor you will probably be the only member of staff to have a genuine overview of how a student is doing across subjects and socially. Use the data to support your work with students.

The whole-person approach

It is part of your role as form tutor to set targets with students, often with their parents/carers present. Many schools now have AST days (Academic and Social Target setting), where the timetable is replaced by 15 minute interviews with parents/carers and students. Other schools have retained more traditional tutor/parent evenings for this. Use the time to forge links with parents/carers and allow them to set at least one of the targets themselves for their child.

You also need to avoid drowning parents/carers in data that means a lot to you, but nothing to them! So look at developing friendly, student-based targets.

The whole-person approach

Some target setting can be done in tutor time. It is useful to work with students before the actual set day or time by getting them to rough out targets on paper in quiet moments in registration etc. You can then collect these in to read or annotate to help the students. This will show the students that targets are important and that you are taking an interest in how they are shaped. It will also allow you to work with students to set realistic and useful targets. *This will help you establish a culture of support for your tutees*, and they will start engaging you in chats linked to their own educational development.

Targets to avoid

It is easy to fall into setting nice-sounding, but difficult-to-monitor targets. One classic is *'concentrate harder in lessons'*. Without being linked to a specific grade or teacher comment goal, it is unmeasurable – unless you wire the student up to a brain scanner!

Try to look for practical, focused targets that are easy to evaluate.
Aim always for SMART targets:

Specific   **Measurable**   **Achievable**   **Relevant** **Time-related**

Useful targets

If you think in threes it helps! Try one target for the student's best or favourite subject, one for the least favourite/hardest, and one which the parents or student offer. A useful target is for a student to commit to seeing a certain teacher by a definite date. This helps open a dialogue between student and teacher, as well as making the student take some responsibility for their learning/development.

Examples:
'See Ms. Smith about my geography work by the end of next week.'
'Get at least grade B for all my science work this term.'
'Don't get any detentions this half-term.'
'Bring equipment to all P.E. lessons this month.'
'Keep my art sketch book up to date.'
'Do my history homework on the day it is set.'
'Remember my day book every day this term.'

Notice that all are specific and time related. They are also easy to monitor, and are linked to academic or social development.

Follow-up

Most schools will have a rolling programme of target reviews at set points of the school year. If not, make sure you regularly talk with your tutees about their targets. You need to bring targets out of folders and under students' noses. One way is to get each student to pick one key target and then write it out to pin up in the tutorial room. One colleague has his form's targets pinned around the door so that students see them every day on their way out. Another idea is to collate the form's targets in one A4 folder that you refer to in form time to talk to students one-to-one at the front of the room.

Targets will only work if you follow them up!

Ideas
for Tutorials

Changing roles

As schools move away from older models of PSHE delivery, you may well find yourself experiencing different requirements as you move between jobs.

- Some schools have transferred the delivery of pastoral content completely from form tutors to a dedicated pastoral team. But if you are committed to pastoral care, it would be a positive move to join the pastoral team
- Some schools have elements of pastoral teaching firmly embedded within the form tutor role
- Some schools will allow a form tutor to use registration time as the tutor sees fit

You will be given materials and details of areas to cover with your tutor group from your line manager. The suggestions that follow are simply aimed at giving you ideas to build on, whatever kind of school you are working in.

Personalise the form room

Use tutor time to forge a sense of class identity, as well as to boost student self-esteem and awareness. A simple way to do this involves students making 'personality profile' displays for their form room.

- Give each student an A4 blank sheet
- Invite them to cover it in a montage of pictures/photos/fabrics that relate to their personal likes in music/fashion/films etc. But they should keep the finished display anonymous
- Display them in the room and invite other classmates to identify who each profile represents

If you can, store the displays at the end of the year and get students to review their own tastes annually, redoing their personality displays each year. This is very amusing and allows students to see how their tastes change as they grow up!

Personality presentations

Get your tutees to make presentations to the form about topics they are interested in, hobbies, or causes that they feel should be supported. This will help students see their classmates as more rounded people rather than people they vaguely know. Use the talks to stimulate wider discussion of issues, and even get the whole form to adopt a charitable cause highlighted by one of the presentations.

You could also set up a class scrap book, where interesting aspects of each student presentation are stored as an archive for reference.

Supporting literacy

Reading mornings
You can support literacy as well as citizenship by cultivating the idea of 'reading registrations'. It may be possible to start this off yourself by visiting bargain bookshops and setting up a small reading library of a dozen or so titles in your form room. Add to this by bringing in a couple of newspapers for students to read. Pick one registration a week to be a reading morning, where students can access the books, newspapers, or bring in something to read themselves.

Spelling challenges
You can also set up simple 10 word spelling tests, the words from which students then have to develop into a paragraph.

Two-minute talks
These can be based on books that students have read, or general interest/news items. Students have to make quick two-minute presentations to their partners, tables, or whole class.

Developing general knowledge

Quizzes

One creative and fun way of using registration/tutor time is to divide the class into quiz teams and keep a running score, on the wall, of how the teams are doing as you run quizzes over the year.

There are many ways to go about this, but an easy starting point is to buy a cheap quiz book and use that. As the year develops, you could ask each team to submit questions to the rest of the class. Alternatively, you could set up current affairs questions to support citizenship and the development of general knowledge.

Using music

Buying an inexpensive radio-CD player is a sure-fire way of bonding with your form! You can use it to encourage music time. Over the year, ask each student to bring in a favourite piece of music to listen to in tutor time/registration (and don't forget to inflict your own choices on the form too!).

As a brief intro get the student to explain why they have chosen the track to be played. It may also be possible to get discussion going after each piece about the quality of the music, but be prepared for frank exchanges of views!

Study time

If you are a lower school tutor, it may be useful to allow students to work on homework during a period of registration or tutorial that you set up as 'study time'. During this time encourage students to reflect on different pieces of academic work they have done. This may well also open up opportunities for discussion on specific topics, or about assessment methods.

Use this time to model different revision techniques:

- Get the students to make revision cards with a picture on one side and text on the back
- Model a brainstorm summary on the board and then get students to do their own
- Encourage students to make up rhymes and songs linked to revision content
- Pair up students to write mnemonics

Study time

You can support older students in their GCSE and examination work by creating a period of study time where they can develop ongoing work. This will also help you oversee progress and show your tutees that you can support their learning across all subjects.

*   Help your students by giving advice on examination timing – get them to work to a set time to see how they manage time pressure

*   Set up a discussion where students can contribute different ideas on how to revise. Collate the ideas on a handout

*   Look at ways to deal with stress – build some work around these questions: 'What does exam stress feel like?'; 'Can you think of three ways to deal with exam stress?'; 'How would you advise next year's examination classes to cope with the stress of exams?'

*   Focus on success to encourage tutees. Ask them what makes them successful as learners – make each student say something positive!

Current affairs time

You can support citizenship by using some tutor time to discuss a topic currently in the news. Students can be encouraged to bring in news articles etc. linked to the discussion topic. From here, you could get the form to:

- Set up surveys asking other students and each other about the events in the news
- Summarise the news into a booklet or presentation for a younger class
- Put together a role-play showing the main parts of the story

Alternatively, you could set up each table as a newsroom with the task of preparing a news broadcast on the topic.

Creating regular 'current affairs time' will also allow you and your form to explore more tragic or sensitive issues in the news.

Debates

One way of supporting whole-school 'thoughts for the week' and citizenship work is to set up a formal class debate over a chosen issue such as animal rights or tolerance.

You will need to set up the activity carefully. You could set up 'for', 'against' and 'neutral' tables. On each table set out prepared materials for students' use, then allocate students to tables and explain they have to argue the point of view of the table, which will not necessarily reflect their own feelings. The neutral tables listen and then vote on the debate.

Another approach is to let the students select which table to sit at and to bring in materials themselves to use in the debate. You can usefully be employed as a non-voting chair in such debates!

Holidays

At the start of new terms or half-terms you can get students to talk about and show things from their holidays.

- You could put up a map of the world or of Britain and mark on it where members of the form have been

- You could encourage students to bring in a postcard from where they have been and collate a form collage

- Students who didn't go away can talk about aspects of their holiday time, such as socialising they have done, films they have seen or relatives visited

What Do
They Want
from Me?

 Routines
and Admin

 Working with
Parents and
Carers

 Pastoral
and Social
Development

 Effective
Target
Setting

 Ideas for
Tutorials

 Professional
Development

Professional
Development

Training and courses

You will want to develop your tutoring skills through in-service training and courses. Use your line manager as a guide to which courses will best suit you, but keep an eye out for ones focused on areas such as:

Target setting
Bereavement
Child protection
Mentoring
Citizenship
Bullying
Counselling

Look to develop your **career** as a form tutor through attendance on courses, in the same way that you develop your career as a subject teacher.

Career options

You could develop a career as a **pastoral leader**, in which case you could follow the path of taking on a pastoral line manager responsibility, typically a head of year role. You would then move to more senior roles linked to whole-school pastoral work such as managing the transition between years, or child protection responsibilities.

Alternatively you may aim to specialise with one particular year group. Some schools have a fixed year 7 tutor team, who have honed the skills of settling new students into school life and routines. In other schools you may well be able to specialise as part of the key stage 4 teams or at sixth form level.

You will also deal with a number of outside agencies as a tutor, for matters such as careers, social care and support, drama productions for life skills, and talks linked to the delivery of aspects of a PSHE programme. Working with these agencies can give you some useful ideas for your own development, as well as new approaches to use with your form.

Training audit

Use this as a guide to identify your training needs as a form tutor.

	Very confident	Fairly confident	Unsure	Very unsure
Delivering PSHE content				
Delivering citizenship				
Dealing with arguments				
Dealing with confidential issues				
Bereavement support				
Organising/running trips for the form				
Writing reports				
Interviewing parents/carers				
Dealing with outside agencies				

Further reading

How to be a Successful Form Tutor
by A Orton and R Rogers. Published by Continuum, 2004

Helping Children Cope with the Loss of a Loved One: A Guide for Grown Ups
by W Kroen and P Espeland. Published by Free Spirit Publishing Inc., 1996

Help Me Say Goodbye: Activities for Helping Kids Cope when a Special Person Dies
by J Silverman. Published by Fairview Press, 1999

The Form Tutor (Blackwell Studies in PSE and Pastoral Care)
by P Griffiths and K Sherman. Published by Nelson Thornes, 1991

The Stop Bullying Pocketbook
by Michele Elliott. Published by Teachers' Pocketbooks, 2005

The Trips & Visits Pocketbook
by Jane West. Published by Teachers' Pocketbooks, 2004

www.ofsted.gov.uk (Document Reference HMI 2125)
'Promoting and Evaluating Pupils' Spiritual, Moral, Social and Cultural Development.'

www.kidscape.org.uk

About the author

Roy Watson-Davis

Roy Watson-Davis has 13 years' teaching experience, the last four as a history AST. He has supported initial teacher training and NQT-mentoring for a number of years, and is involved in the development of post-16 teaching and learning across all subjects. He has also helped a school successfully move out of 'special measures'. He recently appeared as a panel member for a number of *'Resource Review'* programmes for Teachers' Television. Roy has developed his form tutoring experience over the last thirteen years as a form tutor to all years from 7-12.

Acknowledgements

This book is dedicated to Paula and Dave

I would like to thank all the staff and students at Blackfen School for Girls in Sidcup. I particularly would like to thank Shelagh Harrison, my pastoral leader for so much of my career, whose support and guidance have shaped so much of how I work as a tutor, and without whom this book could not have been written. I find inspiration in many quarters, so thanks also go to my cats Buster and Mitch; Simon and Anne at DPAS Towers; the music of Deep Purple, Motorhead, and Fairport Convention; Tom Baker and the late Jon Pertwee.

Order Form

Your details

Name _____

Position _____

School _____

Address _____

_____

_____

Telephone _____

Fax _____

E-mail _____

VAT No. (EC only) _____

Your Order Ref

Please send me:

		No. copies
Form Tutor's _____	Pocketbook	
_____	Pocketbook	
_____	Pocketbook	
_____	Pocketbook	
_____	Pocketbook	

Order by Post

Teachers'
Pocketbooks

Laurel House, Station Approach
Alresford, Hants. SO24 9JH UK

Order by Phone, Fax or Internet

Telephone: +44 (0)1962 735573
Facsimile: +44 (0)1962 733637
E-mail: sales@teacherspocketbooks.co.uk
Web: www.teacherspocketbooks.co.uk

Pocketbooks